GOING GREEN

John Howson

Wayland

Friends of the Earth

GOING GREEN

AT HOME AND SCHOOL

Editor: Catherine Ellis
Designer: Helen White

First published in 1993 by
Wayland (Publishers) Ltd
61 Western Road, Hove
East Sussex BN3 1JD, England

Text copyright © Friends of the Earth Trust Limited 1993
Artwork copyright © 1993 Wayland (Publishers) Ltd

British Cataloguing in Publication Data
Howson, John
Going Green: At Home and School
I. Title
333.7
ISBN 0-7502-0508-3

Typeset by White Design
Printed and bound by Proost N. V., Belgium
Printed on 100% recycled paper.

The author would like to give special thanks to Stephen Sterling and Joanna Watson for editorial assistance. Also thanks to Neil Verlander, Liz Peltz, Adeela Warley and Sarah Finch.

Picture acknowledgements
The publishers would like to thank the following for permission to use their pictures in this book: Chapel Studios (Zul Mukhida) *cover, title page*, 19; Bruce Coleman Ltd 9 bottom (M.Freeman), 11 bottom (M.Boulton), 13 (C.James), 16 (J.Cowan), 28 (C.James); Mark Edwards/Still Pictures 4, 5 bottom, 21, 26, 40-1, 44; The Environmental Picture Library 7 bottom (G.Burns), 8 bottom (M.Jackson), 9 top (G Burns), 15 (M.Bond), 22 top (D.Townend), 25 (M. Bond), 30 (V.Miles), 31 bottom (D.Christelis), 39 inset (R.Hadley), 40 inset (N.Dickinson), 42 (C.Macpherson), 45 (R.Brook); Eye Ubiquitous 18 (Paul Seheult); Friends of the Earth 33 (M. Birkin); NHPA 5 top (L.Campbell), 22 bottom (J.Shaw), 31 top (D.Woodfall); Planet Earth 41 inset (M.Clay); Topham 39 left; Tony Stone Worldwide 6 (O.Benn), 12-13 (M.Lambert), 14 (L.Bradley), 23 (G.Fritz) 34-5 (L.Rhodes); Zefa 7 top, 11 top, 20, 34 inset, 36; Wayland Picture Library 8 top, 24.
Cover artwork by Maureen Jackson.
Inside artwork by John Davey.

CONTENTS

INTRODUCTION
by Jonathon Porritt 4

GETTING GOING
Your area 6
A tale of four young people 8
Your home 10

RECYCLING
Why recycle? 13
A world apart 16
Buying recycled goods 19

POLLUTION
Air pollution 22
Saving the ozone layer 26
Water pollution 30
Pollution alert 33

ENERGY
Energy and you 34
Global warming 37

HABITATS
Tropical rainforests 40
Going green in the garden 42
Wildlife garden 43

WHAT NEXT?
Making changes 44

GLOSSARY 46

FURTHER INFORMATION 47

INDEX 48

INTRODUCTION

↑ These children in Sri Lanka are going to plant trees on deforested land.

HAVE you ever heard of the Children's Crusade? Back in 1212, at the time of the crusades, many thousands of children in France and Germany decided to try to bring an end to those bloody battles by sailing off to the Holy Land to convert Muslims to Christianity – peacefully, rather than by the power of the sword. As you might guess, their crusade was a total failure. Most of the children died on the way, or were sold into slavery.

Hardly a glorious moment in the history books! But I sometimes think that what we need today is another children's crusade, with all children united in one common purpose on behalf of Planet Earth. Just think of thousands of children, from every country in the world, rising up and demanding that their governments start taking action *now* to deal with today's ecological crisis.

You have probably heard of some of the ecological problems facing the earth – global warming, world poverty, ozone depletion, population growth, famine, loss of forests, extinction of species, over-fishing, soil erosion, toxic wastes – the list goes on and on. Even today's politicians agree that all is not quite well with the world.

The sad truth is that decisions being made by adults (or not made!) will have a serious impact on *you*. Most of us keep putting off until tomorrow what should be done today.

But the whole purpose of this book is to show that you're not powerless. There is so much you can do.

First Get informed. Find out the facts, ask questions, take nothing for granted.

Second Get stuck in to the small-scale changes which you can make in your own life and persuade others to make in theirs.

← The tree of life at the Earth Summit in Rio de Janeiro, June 1992.

▶ We need to preserve the earth's natural environment for future generations.

Third Get together with others in your school, or join local or national environmental organizations.

All this really does matter. These days, we tend to hear a great deal about the bad news, but it would be wrong to ignore the good news. Many people are already hard at work tackling the ecological crisis – in schools, in the business community, through scientific research, in our homes, and in the minds and spirits of millions of people around the world.

So we're not quite starting from scratch. But the earth needs your generation to speed up the process of change, to put pressure on adults, to make your voices heard. It's never too late, but the longer we delay, the harder it will get.

Jonathon Porritt
Jonathon Porritt was director of Friends of the Earth between 1984-90. He appears regularly on BBC's *Going Live*.

GETTING GOING

YOUR AREA

Going green – what does it mean? It means thinking and caring about the environment, and living so we don't damage it. This book is an action guide, and at the same time an introduction to the issues you'll need to know about if you're going to be green.

So, where do you start? Many environmental issues appear big and complicated, and beyond our control. But in fact, often we can make a difference, right now, and right where we are. Let's see how.

▲ Motorway madness. Every day there are millions of cars on the roads, giving out huge amounts of waste gases.

The best place to start looking for solutions to environmental problems is in your own home, school or town, because what you, your family and friends do affects the world. Things like the kind of furniture you buy affects precious wildlife habitats in rainforests. If you simply remember to turn off the light in an empty room you will be saving energy and, as you will see, reducing pollution.

Often global, or world, problems are caused by thousands or even millions of local problems put together. This is certainly true in the case of pollution.

▲ If you can, it is better to walk to school rather than go in the car.

Think about your journey to school. You probably notice traffic jams (particularly if they make you late for school), and smell car exhaust fumes filling the air. If you pass a factory you may notice fumes from the chimney. Every day, all over the world, thousands of local power stations and millions of cars pour out huge amounts of waste gases into the atmosphere. Each individual car adds to this pollution.

Scientists think that the changes in the earth's atmosphere caused by some types of pollution are likely to cause the world's temperature to increase. This is known as global warming. Of course, you can't see the effects of global warming in your neighbourhood. But what happens locally, and what happens globally are closely related.

Quite often, by helping to solve local problems you can also help solve some of the global ones. For example, if you walk or cycle to school, instead of going by car, you are helping to reduce the number of cars on the road in your town. You are also helping avoid the pollution problems caused by the car.

Other local issues are special to one area. For example, plans to build a new road might threaten a particular woodland. Local campaigns can often save areas of natural habitat. This was the case in Stroud, in Gloucestershire, where action by a local Friends of the Earth group helped save a group of trees from being cut down. Whether you are campaigning to save one tree or a whole rainforest, your action could make all the difference.

▲ Young campaigners against toxic waste in Scotland.

A TALE OF FOUR YOUNG PEOPLE

There are many ways to help solve environmental problems. What you can do will partly depend on where you live, but everyone can get involved in protecting the environment.

Sarah, James, Matthew and Teira are four young people who live in very different circumstances. Here are their stories.

JAMES

James lives in a block of flats in a large city. His mother works in a local supermarket. James is very interested in wild animals, especially birds. From his bedroom window, he often watches a kestrel which hovers over an area of waste land next to his flat. Every morning, on his way to school, James looks out for some squirrels that live in the trees beside the road. Although the area where James lives is full of houses and cars, some wildlife manages to survive.

James is worried about the animals that are becoming extinct all over the world and would like to do something to help. What can he do?

SARAH

Sarah lives in the far north of England on the edge of the Scottish borders. Her father works on a local farm. He is one of the few skilled shepherds left in the area and his services are much in demand. Sarah thinks that she is very lucky because she has a house overlooking a valley.

▶ BELOW James would like to do something to help protect wildlife.

▶ BOTTOM Sarah lives just near a large peatbog like this one.

Like James, Sarah is fond of animals. She is worried about pollution and the destruction of animals' habitats. The local stream has fewer fish in it than it had a few years ago, and it is known that the area suffers from acid rain. Just a few minutes walk from Sarah's home is a large peatbog that is being drained for trees to be planted there. The peatbog is home to many plants and animals, some of which are quite rare. Sarah likes to go for walks to the edge of this area whenever she can. How can she help save the peatbog?

GOING GREEN

MATTHEW

Matthew lives on a housing estate on the edge of a small town. Both he and his parents are very concerned about problems of the environment and do what they can to help. Matthew is particularly worried about water pollution. One of his favourite places is a stream not far from his house. He has also been interested in recycling ever since he made some recycled paper at school.

James, Sarah and Matthew all helped to protect the environment in their own way. James started a conservation club at school and helped to raise money for rainforest conservation. Through her parents, Sarah heard about a group trying to save the peatbog. She and her mother went along to several of their meetings, and now they have become involved in the struggle. Matthew has started to collect paper for recycling.

▲ Matthew loves studying things in the stream near his house.

◄ Teira's family have been forced to move deeper into the forest to find food to survive.

TEIRA

Teira is quite different from James, Sarah and Matthew. She lives in the rainforest in the Amazon. Her family have lived there happily for generations. Teira's family know how to live with the forest in a way that preserves it for the future. Although they cut down small areas of the forest to grow their crops, the trees soon grow back when the tribe moves on to a new area of rainforest. Teira loves the creatures of the forest, and knows a lot about how they live together. Her parents have taught her how to live by making use of the animals and plants in the forest around her.

Teira's family live in a very remote area, but not far from where they live the forest is being burnt down. People want to use the land for farming and cattle-ranching.

Teira's home and way of life are under threat. But we can help save her way of life by taking action here in Britain.

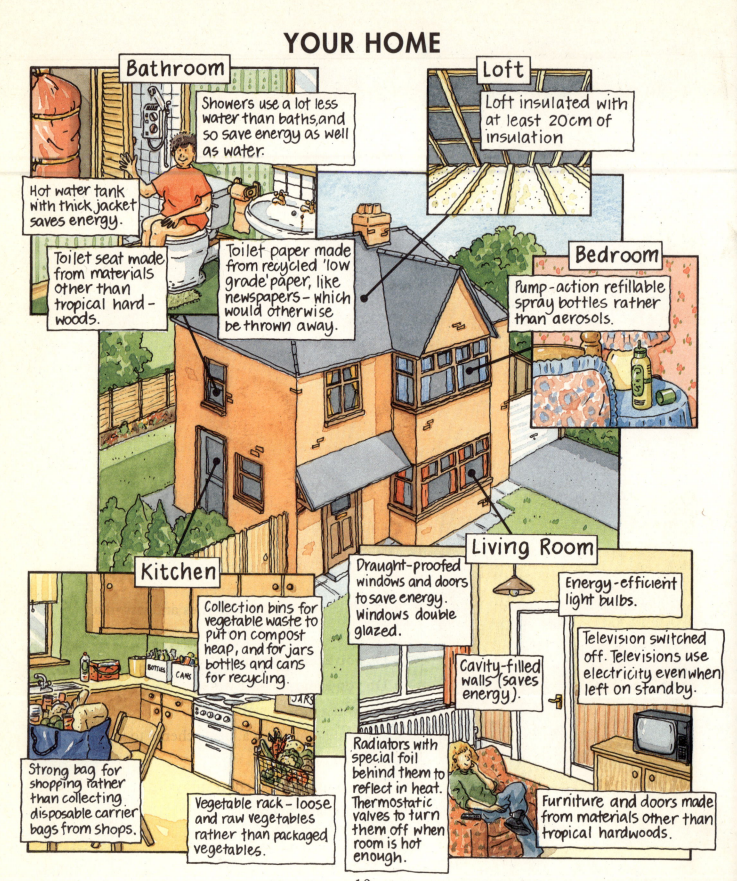

If you want to help the environment outdoors, the best place to start, funnily enough, is indoors. There's a lot that you can do in your own home that will help save the environment. From the things you buy, to the way you use energy (for washing, heating, lighting, running a car), the way you live makes a difference to the environment.

The picture opposite shows a house that has been designed to reduce its effect on the environment.

◄ Tropical timber is used for many things, such as front doors.

▶ Having a shower can use a lot less water than a bath, and so save both water and energy.

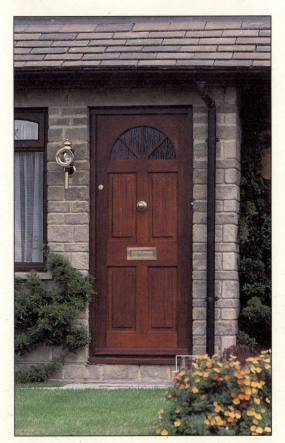

SURVEY
YOU AND YOUR AREA

At the end of each chapter in this book there is a survey to help you find out how well you are doing at going green. The surveys are starting points. First answer the questions yourself, then ask your family and friends. You might like to add questions of your own too.

- Do you put your cans, bottles and jars in a bottle bank to be recycled?
- Do you avoid dropping litter?
- Do you avoid wasting water?
- Are you a member of a conservation group?
- Are you involved in a local scheme to improve the environment?
- Do you use pump-action sprays?
- Do you have a compost heap?

GOING GREEN

RECYCLING

◆ Every year millions of tonnes of waste are buried in landfill sites such as this one.

← BELOW RIGHT
Recycling paper saves energy and prevents waste.

WHY RECYCLE?

What a load of rubbish! The average family in Britain throws away one tonne of rubbish every year. In the USA the figure is even higher.

Just think what would happen if our bins were not collected. Within a short time, huge piles of rubbish would build up on streets and in people's gardens. There would be rats and mice everywhere. People's health would soon be at risk and there would be a public outcry.

It is easy to forget about your rubbish as soon as it has been collected. But where does it all go? And what happens to it?

Nine out of every ten binfulls of our rubbish end up being buried in big holes in the ground called landfill sites. These sites can cause serious pollution. Liquids from the waste form a 'leachate'. This is a mixture of liquids which leak into the ground. Leachate can be very damaging if it gets into rivers or underground drinking water sources. Natural habitats in rivers and lakes are damaged, and drinking water can become polluted.

Another problem with landfill sites is that the rotting rubbish produces dangerous gases, such as methane. Methane is highly explosive, and is one of the gases that scientists believe may cause the world's climate to change.

GOING GREEN

▲ This pile of crushed tins is ready to be recycled.

WHAT A WASTE

As well as causing pollution, throwing away so much rubbish is very wasteful. Because we throw away so much, new materials are always having to be harvested or mined, and then processed in factories. This uses a lot of energy, causes pollution, and it is using up the earth's precious natural resources. Supplies of natural resources such as oil will eventually run out.

So, what can be done to save materials and reduce pollution? The best solution is to reuse things. Old unwanted clothes and furniture can be repaired and passed on to someone else, and some packaging – like milk bottles – can be reused many times. If something can't be reused, the material it is made from could be recycled into a new product.

Recycling takes up less energy than producing things from raw materials, and it reduces waste. For example, it can take 70 per cent less energy to recycle paper than to make paper from virgin pulp. Recycling aluminium cans can save up to 96 per cent of the energy used to make new cans. Also, did you know that by recycling your aluminium cans you may be helping to protect wildlife? This is because tropical rainforest habitats are sometimes destroyed to get aluminium.

A lot of things that are often thrown away could be recycled. For example, toilet paper can be made from recycled newspapers, instead of the good quality waste paper that is usually used. If more people bought recycled paper toilet rolls, more would be made, and fewer old newspapers would have to be dumped in landfill sites.

REUSE, RECYCLE

There are things we can all do to avoid waste. At least half the things most people throw away could be reused or recycled. Clothes, furniture and household goods could all be repaired or given to charity shops and jumble sales. Other items, such as glass, metals, paper, textiles and even plastics, can be recycled.

The British government has set a target of recycling 25 per cent of all household rubbish by the end of this century. In 1991 less than 3 per cent was recycled, so a lot of improvement is needed. Many councils still do not have adequate facilities for recycling, and say they can't afford to set them up.

▲ Recycling CFCs helps to protect the ozone layer, but only a tiny amount is currently recovered by councils.

TAKING ACTION

Contact your local authority to find out where your local recycling facilities are. If the council does not have any facilities for recycling your waste, you could write a letter to the council asking them why not.

A WORLD APART

Next time you go to the shop to buy something, try asking yourself, 'Do I really need this?' Having many possessions – clothes, tools, furniture, cars, bicycles, toys, videos – is a luxury only common in the richer nations of the world. In poor countries, people have to use their possessions much more carefully, and repair them when they get old rather than replace them.

In the past, most towns and villages in Britain had workshops where you could take things to be mended. Many department stores used to have repair sections too. Today it is often difficult to get things repaired when they wear out. Shops want you to buy new things rather than repair the old.

▲ An umbrella repairer in India. Some societies use materials less wastefully than others.

The bar chart below shows how much rubbish the average person produces every day in various parts of the world. You will notice that the poorer countries produce less waste per person than the richer countries.

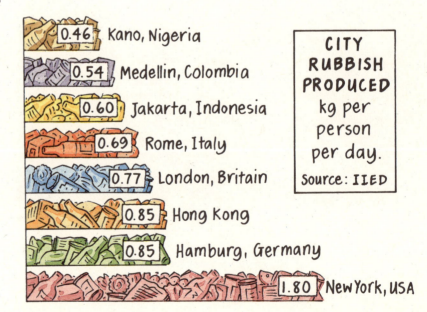

CITY RUBBISH PRODUCED kg per person per day. Source: IIED

0.46 Kano, Nigeria
0.54 Medellin, Colombia
0.60 Jakarta, Indonesia
0.69 Rome, Italy
0.77 London, Britain
0.85 Hong Kong
0.85 Hamburg, Germany
1.80 New York, USA

As well as some countries throwing away more than others, the kind of things they throw away differs too. The pie charts on the right show the difference between what people throw away in Jakarta and in London. Why do you think there is such a difference?

Below is a picture of what is in an ordinary family's dustbin in Britain, showing how much of it can be recycled or reused.

LONDON
55% – paper, metal, glass and plastic
15% – other waste
30% – organic waste

JAKARTA
10% – other waste
10% – paper, metal, glass and plastic
80% – organic waste

Glass
10% of household waste. Ideally glass jars and bottles should be returned for reuse. They can also be reused at home, or recycled through bottle banks or recycling collections.

Kitchen and garden waste
33% of household waste. Most can be recycled by composting.

Plastic
7% of household waste. Plastic containers should be reused. If they can't be reused, they should be recycled.

Paper and Card
30% of household waste. Most card and paper can be recycled through paper banks, or a recycling collection scheme.

Metal
10% of household waste. Much can be recycled. Separate it into iron (ferrous) and aluminium using a magnet. (Aluminium will not stick to a magnet.)

Other (eg: shoes, plant pots, ashes, dust)
10% of household waste. Much of this is difficult to recycle.

Going Green

SURVEY
RUBBISH

An awful lot of our rubbish can be reused or recycled. Take a piece of paper and make a list of all of the things that you throw away in one week. In a second column, put a tick by the things that could have been recycled. Which things do you think may be difficult to recycle and why? Could you have avoided using any of them in the first place? Can you think of any ways in which manufacturers could make things easier to recycle?

DOOR-TO-DOOR COLLECTIONS

One of the best ways to get a lot of people to recycle their rubbish is for the local council to organize a doorstep collection scheme. Householders put their rubbish for recycling in special bins to be collected. The dustcarts are divided into sections so that recyclables can be kept separate. By organizing this sort of scheme councils can collect more material than through using recycling banks to which people have to take their own rubbish.

➤ One of Adur district council's doorstep collection lorries. Councils are responsible for collecting recyclable waste.

Going Green

BUYING RECYCLED GOODS

So, you've started to collect things for recycling. What next? As well as recycling waste it is important that people also buy the resulting products. Nowadays you can buy lots of things made from recycled materials, such as envelopes, photocopying paper and this book! People often think that goods made from recycled material are more expensive, but this is not always true. The more people buy products made from recycled material, the more factories will make them – and the cheaper they will become. Recycled paper is now much cheaper than it was when it first appeared in shops, and sometimes it is cheaper than non-recycled paper.

⬆ What you buy can make a difference! The more people buy products made from recycled materials, such as these recycled toilet rolls, the more manufacturers will make them.

TAKING ACTION

You and your friends could get together and start a recycling scheme for your school. Ask your teachers to help.

A lot of the high quality paper your school uses is ideal for recycling, but low quality paper can be recycled too. Does your school reuse things like paper and envelopes, bottles, jars and so on?

Cans, glass and plastics can also be recycled. Your school could ask the local council to pick up the different materials you collect.

▲ Look at your weekly shopping. How much of the packaging is really necessary?

Don't forget the 'Four Rs' of recycling:

1. **REFUSE** – unnecessary packaging.
2. **REUSE** – everything you can.
3. **REPAIR** – rather than buying new equipment.
4. **RECYCLE** – waste paper, cans, glass and so on.

Why not design and decorate some boxes for storing things to be reused or recycled. Use them in your bedroom or kitchen at home, or in your classroom.

SURVEY

RECYCLING

This survey will give you some ideas of what you could be doing to produce less waste. How well do you score?

- Do you buy things made from recycled paper – such as letter paper, exercise books, toilet paper and tissues?
- If you have a garden, does your family make compost from vegetable and garden waste? Does your school have a compost heap?
- Do you reuse packaging wherever possible (for example plastic bags, cardboard boxes), and refuse unnecessary packaging?
- Do you use refillable containers wherever possible?
- Do you repair old clothes and electrical goods, or pass them on to charity shops for reuse or recycling?
- Do you collect any of the following for recycling: newspaper/other paper, glass, cans/metal, plastic, textiles?
- Do you buy milk in returnable bottles, and return them?

If you don't do all of these yet don't worry. The list is intended to give you some idea of what you can do.

➤ You can help reduce pollution by recycling waste at school. These pupils have built can crushers.

POLLUTION

AIR POLLUTION

If you had lived in London in the 1950s you would have been very aware of air pollution. The coal that people burned on fires in their homes and in factories caused horrible thick fogs, known as smogs or 'pea soupers'. Sometimes you could hardly see where you were going. Some of these smogs were very dangerous. Up to 4,000 people died as a result of one famous smog in 1952. Cattle at Smithfield Market also died, and dockers reported smog so thick they couldn't see their feet!

In 1956, the government passed a law called the Clean Air Act. This meant councils could declare smoke-free zones. Nowadays British cities suffer from another kind of pollution.

▲ Many cyclists now wear masks to protect themselves from traffic pollution.

▶ RIGHT Acid rain can damage trees. When certain gases mix with water droplets in clouds, they cause acid rain.

▶ OPPOSITE A blanket of smog over New York City. Smogs like this are increasingly common in cities around the world.

The smogs that pollute the air in our cities and towns today are less visible than the old pea soupers, but they are still bad for our health. Gases such as nitrogen oxide and hydrocarbons, which make smog, are given off when fossil fuels are burned. (Fossil fuels are things like coal, oil and natural gas.) These gases can react in strong sunlight and give off the gas ozone, one of the worst ingredients of modern smog. You have probably heard that ozone is needed in the 'ozone layer', but it is not needed at ground level. It is a very harmful pollutant and is particularly bad for people who suffer from asthma and bronchitis.

GOING GREEN

23

Burning fossil fuels in cars is one of the biggest causes of smog. Cars also produce many other types of pollution, such as benzene (which escapes from petrol tanks) and the poisonous gas carbon monoxide. Fumes from petrol that contains lead are especially harmful too.

Pollution is not only caused by cars. Many power stations which burn fossil fuels give off harmful gases like sulphur dioxide and nitrogen oxide. When these gases mix with the water droplets in clouds they cause acid rain. Acid rain is damaging to both animals and plants.

PREVENTING AIR POLLUTION

To reduce pollution we need to do two things: we need to find ways of using less energy, and we need to find cleaner ways of producing energy.

For example, think about how you get to school – by car, bus, train, bicycle? If thirty people travel by bus instead of going separately in cars, that means thirty fewer cars on the roads. And that means less pollution per person. Even better would be thirty people going by bike! Unfortunately, many of our busy roads are dangerous places for cyclists and pedestrians. But they

◂ If more people travelled by bus, instead of by car, there would be less pollution.

TAKING ACTION

If your parents decide to buy a new car, try to persuade them to buy one with a catalytic convertor. Avoid asking them to give you lifts in the car unless it is really necessary, and encourage them to travel by bus or train more often.

If you live near a road that is dangerous for cyclists, why not write to your local council and ask them to make it safer?

Find out how many of your teachers share lifts or cycle to school. Suggest to them that doing either of these would be a good way of saving energy.

could be made safer. Building special cycle lanes by the side of roads, and forcing traffic to slow down in built-up areas are methods used with great success in Holland and Denmark.

Another way to cut down on pollution is to fit car exhausts with special filters called catalytic convertors. These can reduce the amount of harmful gases given out by up to 90 per cent. But fitting catalytic convertors is not a solution to all the traffic problems we face. The only long-term solution is to have fewer cars on the road.

If we used less energy, power stations would not have to produce so much, and that would mean less pollution from power stations. Another way to reduce pollution from power stations is to try to get energy in other ways. It is possible to generate electricity from the power of the wind, waves, and sun. These are called renewable sources of energy. Getting electricity from them produces far less pollution than burning fossil fuels.

◆ Developing renewable sources of energy, such as wind power, will help reduce pollution.

SAVING THE OZONE LAYER

Most people these days will have heard of the 'hole' in the ozone layer, but what does this mean, and what can you do to help?

Up in the atmosphere, between 10 and 50 km above the surface of the earth, there is a layer of gas called ozone. Ozone is poisonous at ground level, but up in the sky the ozone layer protects life on earth. It does this by soaking up almost all of the damaging ultraviolet (UV) radiation given off by the sun. UV radiation can cause skin cancers and eye disease. It also harms plants and animals.

▲ Ozone depletion increases the risk of developing skin cancer.

The story of the 'hole' began in 1984, when scientists working in the Antarctic found an area in the upper atmosphere where there was far less ozone than there ought to have been. This 'hole' was as big as the USA. It appeared every spring.

Scientists have discovered that certain chemicals released into the atmosphere by humans are destroying the ozone layer. One of the most harmful groups of chemicals is known as CFCs, or chlorofluorocarbons. Other harmful chemicals are HCFCs (Hydro-chlorofluorocarbons) and halons.

TAKING ACTION

CFCs are most commonly used in fridges, freezers and air conditioners. It is possible to remove the CFCs from these and recycle the gas, rather than letting it escape to harm the ozone layer. If your parents are getting rid of an old fridge or freezer ask them to contact your local authority to find out if they can remove the CFCs for recycling. Some shops also remove the CFCs from fridges and freezers. Try to find out what your school does with old fridges and freezers.

The gas halon is often used in fire extinguishers. Check what type of fire extinguisher you have at school. If you have any that contain halon you could suggest to the teachers that they investigate having them replaced.

HUNTING DOWN HALONS

- In the UK most halons are used in hand-held portable fire extinguishers.
- Most halon extinguishers are found near electrical fire hazards, in homes and offices, cars, taxis, buses and trains.
- They are nearly all coloured green.

◆ CFCs are broken apart by the sun's rays, producing chlorine atoms. These atoms react with ozone and make still more chlorine. As this continues, more and more ozone is destroyed.

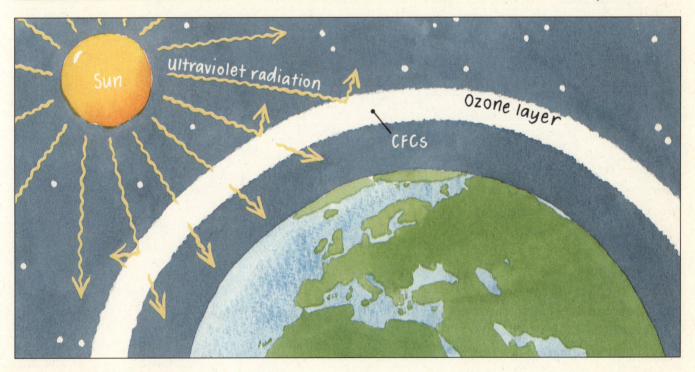

You do not have to live in the Antarctic to be affected by the destruction of the ozone layer. The atmosphere over much of North America, Western Europe and Australia also has less ozone than it ought to. Governments all over the world have now agreed to stop the manufacture of CFCs, but mostly not for some years. We need to get rid of these and other ozone-destroying chemicals as fast as we possibly can, as it will take a long time for the ozone layer to recover.

◄ CFCs can be recovered from old fridges. This helps save the ozone layer.

SURVEY
REDUCING AIR POLLUTION

As well as carrying out this survey yourself, why not get your friends and teachers to complete it too?

- Do you use a bike or share lifts to school with other children?
- If your parents have a car, is it fitted with a catalytic convertor?
- If your parents have a car, does it run on unleaded petrol?
- Do you use public transport wherever possible instead of travelling by car?
- If your parents have bought a new fridge recently, did they buy a CFC-reduced fridge? When they disposed of the old fridge, did they try to get the CFCs recycled?

TEST FOR FUMES

The following experiment is a good way of finding the level of particulates in your area. Particulates are tiny pieces of carbon that are produced by burning fossil fuels. They can be harmful, particularly for people who suffer from asthma or bronchitis. Try this experiment near to a main road and then try it in an area well away from a road. Do you get different results?

You will need:
scissors, sticky tape, white card.

- Find a holly bush, laurel or any evergreen plant. Choose (but don't pick) leaves that are a year old. These will be a little way down the stems and darker in colour than the bright new leaves.
- Using scissors, cut some strips of sticky tape, and press them down firmly on to two or three leaves.
- Do this on different sides of the plant. Then carefully remove the pieces of sticky tape (don't pull off the leaves!) and stick them on to some white card. Make a note on the card of where each sample was taken.
- You'll probably be surprised by how dirty the strips become, especially those taken from a plant near a main road. If you do the experiment near a factory, you may find that a lot of dust has been picked up on the leaves and sticks to the tape.

WATER POLLUTION

Without water, all life on earth would cease to exist. It is very important that our streams, rivers and seas are properly cared for and not carelessly polluted, and that the water we drink remains clean and pollution-free. Some rivers in Britain have become so polluted that nothing can live in them.

One of the main causes of pollution in Britain's rivers is sewage. Sewage treatment works remove the solid sewage sludge, and release the remaining liquid into rivers. But our rivers can't cope with the amount that is pumped into them. Some of the chemicals in sewage can damage streams and their wildlife. Waste from farms and chemicals from industry also pollute rivers and streams.

HEALTHY WATERS?

Did you know that swimming in the sea can be bad for your health? In Britain alone, 1,364 million litres of untreated or partly-treated sewage is poured into the sea every day. Bacteria and viruses from the sewage can make people ill. There is a European law which sets standards for bathing water, but not all seaside areas and rivers meet them. If you want to know whether a beach meets the legal pollution standards, ask the local council.

▶ Sewage on Blackpool beach. Many of Britain's beaches are polluted.

⬆ It is important that our rivers and streams are properly cared for, and not carelessly polluted.

▶ Clean drinking water is vital for our health.

DRINKING WATER

Having clean, pure water to drink is vital for our health. In Britain in the nineteenth century, many people used to die from diseases such as typhoid as a result of drinking dirty water. Nowadays, in countries like Britain where water is treated, typhoid is almost unknown. But instead there is a different threat to people's health. Small amounts of chemicals, such as pesticides and nitrates, get into our drinking water. Although the amount of these chemicals in our water is often very small, there may be more than is allowed under European law.

If you are worried about your drinking water, write to your local water company. They must tell you whether your water meets the standards set by law.

POLLUTION ALERT

◀ Young campaigners protest against sewage pollution of Cornish beaches.

TAKING ACTION

If you live near a river or beach it is worth keeping an eye out for signs of pollution, such as dead fish, raw sewage or oil spills. If you do find evidence of pollution, do not touch it as it could make you ill. Unfortunately, by the time these signs appear, much of the damage has already been done. Preventing water pollution from happening in the first place is the most important task.

In England and Wales, you can report incidents of pollution to the National Rivers Authority; in Scotland you can contact the River Protection Board or local Island Council; and in Northern Ireland approach the Environment Protection Division at the Department of the Environment.

You can play your part in preventing pollution by always disposing of harmful substances carefully. People should not, for instance, put old engine oil down the drain.

If your family owns a car, you can ask your parents to take used engine oil to a garage that collects old oil for recycling. Batteries also contain polluting material – so don't leave old ones lying around. Your council may have safe disposal facilities for batteries and other hazardous household waste. Better still, use rechargeable batteries.

GOING GREEN

ENERGY

ENERGY AND YOU

The way we use energy is the cause of many of the earth's environmental problems, such as global warming, acid rain and smog. Few other things that humans do have such a big effect on the earth. If we made better use of our energy supplies, we could use about 70 per cent less energy than we do at the moment. That's a big saving! We could do this and live just as comfortably as we do at the moment, and we would be helping the environment a great deal.

First we need to think about how we use energy. Then we can look for ways to use less.

ENERGY USE IN THE HOME

The energy that we need to do things for us is called useful energy. Unfortunately, whenever we use energy some always gets wasted, or lost. For example, what do you switch lights on for? You'd be very unusual if you said heat, but light bulbs waste energy by giving off heat as well as light.

You can now get special light bulbs which give as much light as an ordinary bulb, but less heat. For this reason they use much less power than a normal light bulb, and are called energy-efficient bulbs – more of the electrical energy they use is turned into useful light energy.

▶ Lighting and heating all the buildings in a city uses up a huge amount of energy. Buildings can be designed to use much less energy.

▼ The house below has solar panels, which will produce energy from the sun's rays.

There are lots of other energy-saving devices available now. If your parents are buying a new appliance for the kitchen, such as a fridge or washing machine, you could suggest they ask the salesperson which uses the least energy.

Some houses are designed so that they capture as much heat from the sun as possible. Building houses like this could save a lot of energy, because the sun's natural energy helps to heat them.

INSULATION

Why do people wear woolly hats in winter? Because the wool traps their natural body heat and keeps them warm. The same idea is used for keeping buildings warm. This is called insulation. A lot of energy is wasted if a building isn't properly insulated because the heat escapes through the roofs, windows, doors and walls.

Most heat is lost through the roofs of buildings, so it is important that a layer of thick material is placed in the loft. You can also get special material to go in the cavity (gap) in the walls. Floors can be insulated by using underlay under carpets. Even putting old newspapers under carpets can help to insulate them. Hot water tanks should have a thick insulating jacket to stop the heat escaping.

Energy can also be saved by stopping draughts that come through badly-fitting doors and windows. Double glazing and curtains with thick linings help to stop draughts from windows. You can also get special strips to fill gaps around doors and windows. Insulating your home and school is a bit like putting them in a woolly jumper. They will be as warm, but use less energy. Investigate how well your home and school are insulated.

Here is a simple experiment that you can do at home or at school to show the usefulness of insulation.

You will need:
two glass jars the same size, water, thermometer, insulating materials (such as cotton wool, rags, newspaper), a small box.

1. Place one jar in a small box surrounded by some insulating material. Make sure it is packed tight in the box.

2. Leave the second jar unwrapped.

3. Fill both jars with the same amount of hot water from the tap.

4. Every five minutes, measure the temperature of each jar of water with a thermometer. Write them down. Do this for half an hour.

5. Look at your results. You could plot them on a graph. Which jar cooled quickest? Can you think of any reasons why the jars cooled at different rates?

Woolly hats help keep us warm, just like insulation helps keep buildings warm.

You can repeat this experiment using different materials to compare their effect as insulators, but make sure that you use the same equipment and the same amount of water heated to the same temperature each time.

GLOBAL WARMING

Have you ever been inside a greenhouse? It is warmer inside than out because the glass traps the heat. Some of the gases in the earth's atmosphere have a similar effect to the glass in a greenhouse. They help to keep the earth warm. This is known as the greenhouse effect, and the gases are known as greenhouse gases. Without them the earth would be over 30 °C cooler, and life as we know it could not exist.

Over the last 100 years, people have been using more and more energy. Most of this energy comes from burning fossil fuels, which give off gases such as carbon dioxide and nitrogen oxides. This pollution is increasing the levels of greenhouse gases in the atmosphere, and this is threatening to raise the earth's temperature.

If you don't like cold weather, you might think that a warmer earth sounds like a good idea. But, the effects of global warming, due to pollution, are not likely to be good news for anyone. Parts of the world that are already very dry may get even less rain, which would cause more famine. Other parts of the world could get more rain. Sea levels would also rise, causing terrible floods.

We must protect the earth from the threat of global warming before it is too late. If we go on burning as much coal, oil and gas as we do at the moment, scientists estimate that the earth's temperature could rise between 1 and 3 °C over the next fifty years. For many parts of the world that would be disastrous.

TAKING ACTION

Did you know that nearly everything you do to save energy will help slow down global warming? Everyone has a role to play in saving energy.

The first rule is, don't use it when you don't have to. For example, whenever a television is left on standby, or lights are left on in an empty room, it not only costs money, it also wastes energy. It means that power stations are burning fossil fuel for nothing. You might think that one television left on standby doesn't use much energy, but multiplied by thousands of televisions, it becomes a lot of wasted energy.

So, save energy when you can. Switch off heaters, lights and any other electrical appliances when you're not using them. In winter, don't expect your house to be so warm that you can walk around in a T-shirt and shorts as if it was summer. Wear jumpers and trousers that will keep you warm. By lowering the thermostat on your central heating by just one degree you could lower your family's fuel bills by up to 10 per cent.

HOW MUCH CARBON DIOXIDE DO YOU PRODUCE?

Carbon dioxide (or CO_2), is the main gas causing global warming. Using the simple calculation on the next page, you can work out approximately how much carbon dioxide your family produces in one week from burning fossil fuels.

1. Electricity is measured in units, and each unit represents 0.83 kg of carbon dioxide. Use your electricity meter at home to record the amount of electricity your family uses during one day. Then multiply this number by seven to work out how many units you use in a week. Now multiply the number of units by 0.83 to work out how much carbon dioxide your family produces from electricity in a week.

Another way to find out how much electricity you use is to look at your quarterly electricity bill. This will tell you how many units you use in three months. Then you can calculate how much carbon dioxide you produce in three months. From that you can work out how much is produced in one week.

2. Gas is measured in therms. Each therm represents 5.85 kg of carbon dioxide. Using your gas meter or gas bill, work out how much carbon dioxide you produce in a week from using gas.

3. Make a record of how much petrol your family car uses during one week. If one litre of petrol produces approximately 2.5 kg of carbon dioxide, how much does your car produce in a week?

4. Now calculate the total amount of carbon dioxide your family produces in one week. If you can find ways to reduce this total, you will be helping to slow down global warming.

SURVEY
ENERGY

This survey is to help you find out how energy-efficient your home and school are. Why not get your neighbours to try it out too?

- Does your school/home have insulation of the roof, walls, floors, hot water tank?
- Do you have double glazing or draught-proofing of doors and windows?
- Does your school/home have energy-efficient light bulbs?
- Do the radiators and heaters at school/home have thermostats?
- Do your parents buy energy-efficient goods where possible (for example, cookers and fridges)?

Now draw up an action plan for 'How to save energy'. You can do some things yourself – such as remembering to turn off lights. Other things you will have to try to persuade your parents and teachers to do. For example, if you think that the school classrooms are overheated, you could suggest that the school fits thermostats to its radiators. This will save the school money too.

GOING GREEN

◀ Global warming could cause terrible flooding in some low-lying countries.

➡ Burning petrol in cars is one of the main sources of carbon dioxide in the atmosphere, which is threatening to cause global warming.

GOING GREEN

HABITATS

TROPICAL RAINFORESTS

Rainforests are precious places. They are home to some of the world's rarest animals and plants. More species of animals and plants live in rainforests than any other habitat on earth. Some of the animals include monkeys, tigers, jaguars, forest elephants and rhinoceroses. Without their rainforest home, these animals and plants cannot survive.

Today, the world's rainforests are in danger. Every year, an area of forest the size of England and Wales (nearly 30 million hectares) is either completely destroyed or badly damaged.

▶ RIGHT Vast areas of rainforest are being destroyed every year.

▶ OPPOSITE A jaguar in the rainforest in Belize. Without their rainforest home, many species of animals and plants could not survive.

▼ BELOW Tribal people protesting about logging in Sarawak, Malaysia.

40

GOING GREEN

The reasons for rainforest destruction are not simple, and there are no quick and easy solutions. But, if this destruction does not stop, there will soon be no rainforests left.

Many rainforest animals and plants are in danger of disappearing forever. Even animals that were once quite common are now becoming scarce. The orang-utan, the woolly spider monkey and many parrot species are all threatened. Many animals, including the Javan tiger and many kinds of bird and butterfly, have already become extinct. That means we will never see them on earth again! It has been estimated that up to fifty species become extinct each day.

So why are the forests being cut down? Over the years, many poor countries have borrowed money from richer countries. To earn money to pay their debts, many countries are cutting down huge areas of their rainforests and selling the timber from the trees. Some forests are burned down to get land to grow crops and graze cattle. The crops and meat are then exported. But rainforest soils are very poor and after a couple of years not much will grow. So then, farmers burn down yet more rainforest. Such huge areas are being burnt each year that the forest is unable to regrow and recover.

WHAT HAVE WE GOT TO LOSE?

The next time you are drinking cola or chewing gum, think of the rainforest – they are made from things originally found there. A lot of valuable products come from the rainforest – many foods and plants, and many medicines and drugs. Every time an area of rainforest is burnt down, undiscovered sources of medicine may be lost.

As well as all the valuable plants and animals, thousands of people live in the world's rainforests. Destroying the forest means destroying their homes. These forest peoples know how to live in the forest without harming it. Their children, like Teira in chapter one, grow up with a deep understanding of the forest as a rich source of natural wealth.

SAVING THE FORESTS

It is not easy to save the rainforests. Environmental organizations, like Friends of the Earth and Survivial International, are trying to stop more rainforests from being cut down by persuading world governments of the need to protect them. One thing you can do is try to persuade people not to buy things that are made from tropical hardwoods, like mahogany, meranti and iroko. These are often used for furniture, doors, window frames and even toilet seats!

GOING GREEN IN THE GARDEN

If you have a garden at home or at school, you've got a golden opportunity to help save the earth! One of the best things you can do is to build a compost heap. Compost is a wonderful natural fertilizer. Simply separate your fruit and vegetable scraps from your other rubbish and begin to make a heap in a corner of the garden. Grass cuttings and weeds should also be put on the pile. This natural waste will gradually rot and produce compost. If there is nowhere you can make a compost heap, try to cut down on the amount of chemicals and fertilizers used, or give them up altogether.

Making compost is much better than throwing food and garden waste away. When this kind of material rots in landfill sites (where there is no oxygen) it produces methane gas, which is explosive and a greenhouse gas. By making your own compost you can avoid using peat. Every year, a huge amount of peat is dug out of peatbogs for people to use in their gardens. Peatbogs are home to many rare animals and plants, but once the bogs are destroyed it is nearly impossible to restore them.

FRIEND OR FOE?

Did you know that although some insects and minibeasts eat your plants, others are natural predators that will protect them? To avoid using polluting pesticides in your garden, you can grow plants that attract natural predators. Making part of your garden into a wild garden, and having a small woodpile are two ways of attracting useful insects. Beetles, ladybirds, hoverflies and lacewings all eat garden pests.

Another way to protect your plants is to place a barrier between the pest and the plant. Putting a fine mesh net over vegetables of the cabbage family (such as broccoli and Brussels sprouts) stops cabbage white butterflies laying their eggs on the plants. The eggs grow into caterpillars that eat the cabbages.

◄ Going green in the garden can be fun.

WILDLIFE GARDEN

Starting your own wildlife garden is one way in which you can play a really active role in improving the environment in your area. But remember, once the garden is set up you will have to maintain it. Wildlife gardens are fun to make and you can learn a lot from watching them develop.

A rubble pile in the shade is a good hiding place for insects, lizards and slow-worms (which eat slugs).

Choose trees that will attract wildlife. Mountain ash and alder grow quickly, producing lots of fruit for birds and other animals. Oaks will feed more wildlife than most trees, but they take 30 years to grow fully.

Certain plants and flowers attract wildlife, like buddleia (excellent for butterflies), nettles, honeysuckle, lavender, clover, poppies and bluebells. Areas of poor, infertile soil are ideal for growing some wild plants.

Mixed hedges will encourage the most wildlife. You could include hawthorn, blackberry, field maple and oak.

A pile of small branches and wood encourages insects and beetles. Birds will eat insects, and beetles will eat the pests in your garden.

Ponds can be expensive and difficult to maintain, but they certainly encourage wildlife, especially frogs. Frogs will eat slugs, and so protect your plants. Choose a site for your pond away from large trees that may clog it with leaves in autumn, and out of direct sunlight.

WHAT NEXT?

MAKING CHANGES

So, you've read about some of the threats to the environment, and have decided you would like to help in the fight to save it. What next?

We can all help protect the environment by being careful about what we buy. Remember the first question you should ask yourself before you buy anything is, 'Do I really need it?' But buying green is not always easy. For a start, there is such a wide range of products available that it's difficult to know which to choose.

Some manufacturers claim that their products are good for the environment just to help sell them. Others have made a real attempt to change how they produce things. A new eco-labelling scheme in the UK awards labels to products that meet certain agreed standards.

Another way to start making changes is to find out about environmental problems that affect your area, and about any local campaigns which might be tackling them. Your local library, and local newspapers are good places to look for information. If you can join or start up a group you'll have more fun and be able to do more. Your group could start a wildlife garden, get your local council to improve its recycling facilities, or map pollution in your local area. You could get in touch with BTCV (British Trust for Conservation Volunteers). See the address section at the back of the book.

One of the most successful ways of protecting the environment is through environmental campaigns.

▲ Children in Canada campaigning to save the Redwood trees.

If you feel very strongly about something, you can write to politicians asking them what they or their parties propose to do about a particular problem. Most politicians take letters that people write very seriously – so writing can really make a difference.

Groups like Friends of the Earth try to persuade people in government and industry to make decisions to help protect the environment. For example they have worked to get companies not to use CFCs.

You or your family might like to join an organization such as Friends of the Earth. Friends of the Earth has a family membership scheme, so all of your family can play a part in protecting the environment. It also has a membership scheme for schools called School Friends which you could encourage your school to join. From this you will receive mailings of useful educational material.

Various organizations have groups for young people which your group at school could join. If you are over 14 this could be an Earth Action group – Earth Action is Friends of the Earth's campaigning youth section.

Finally, you could try raising money to help an environmental campaign group. This can be fun, and you can learn a lot from doing it too. You can raise funds in a number of ways, such as a school fashion show or a sponsored silence. Good luck with going green!

◆ Making a pond can be fun, and they are excellent for attracting wildlife.

GLOSSARY

Acid rain Rain, snow, mist or hail that has been made acidic by waste gases produced by burning fossil fuels.
Carbon dioxide A colourless, odourless gas found in the atmosphere. It can be formed from burning fossil fuels, and contributes to global climate change.
Carbon monoxide A colourless, odourless, very poisonous gas. Like carbon dioxide, it can be formed from burning fossil fuels in vehicles and furnaces.
Catalytic convertor A box fitted to car exhausts that can cut the amount of harmful gases in car exhaust by 90 per cent.
CFCs (chlorofluorocarbons) A group of chemicals that damage the ozone layer.
Climate change The threat of a change to the world's climate by the build up of greenhouse gases in the atmosphere (also known as global warming).
Conservation The protection of nature and natural things.
Emissions Substances let out into the air or water from factories, chimneys and vehicle exhausts.
Fossil fuels Fuels such as oil, coal and natural gas which have formed underground over millions of years from the remains of plants and animals.
Global warming See *climate change*.
Greenhouse effect The effect of gases such as carbon dioxide (CO_2) in the earth's atmosphere, which trap the sun's heat.
Greenhouse gases The name for about thirty gases in the earth's atmosphere that let the sun's heat reach the earth, but stop some of the heat escaping back out to space.
Halons Synthetic chemicals that are mainly used in fire extinguishers. Halons are much more powerful at destroying ozone than CFCs, and have already caused a large amount of the ozone loss over the Antarctic.
Landfill site A place where solid waste is disposed of, usually a hole in the ground.
Nitrates Chemicals that are used in fertilizers to help plants grow. Nitrates can pollute rivers and underground water supplies if they get washed into them.
Nitrogen oxides Gases formed when fossil fuels are burnt at a high temperature. Nitrogen oxides contribute to acid rain. Nitrogen dioxide mixes with oxygen to produce ozone gas.
Nutrients The materials that plants and animals need for growth and life, such as water and minerals.
Organic Any living material. Also a type of farming that does not use artificial chemicals (such as fertilizers and pesticides).
Ozone A gas that forms a vital layer high up in the atmosphere, shielding the earth from the sun's harmful ultraviolet rays. However, ozone is harmful when it occurs near the ground.
Pesticide A chemical used to kill pests, such as insects.
Pollution Damage caused to the environment by substances that are released into it.
Recycling Reprocessing waste materials so that they can be used again.
Renewable energy Sources of energy such as wind and waves, which cannot be exhausted or run out.

Reuse Using materials again without reprocessing, such as milk bottles.
Sewage The waste products and water which are flushed down the drain, toilet or sink.
Smog A mixture of pollutants. Nowadays smogs are formed by nitrogen oxides and hydrocarbons (given out by vehicle exhausts) coming together in strong sunlight.

Sulphur dioxide A colourless gas with a strong odour. It is mainly formed from burning fossil fuels. It is the major cause of acid rain.
Toxic Harmful or poisonous.
Tropical rainforest Thick forest that grows in warm tropical areas, where rainfall is high (2 to 10 m per year) and there is high humidity.

FURTHER INFORMATION

USEFUL ADDRESSES

Please always enclose a stamped address envelope when writing to any of these organizations.

British Trust for Conservation Volunteers, 36 St Mary's Street, Wallingford, Oxfordshire OX10 0EU. (Runs conservation holidays and weekends.)

Centre for Alternative Technology, Llwyngwern Quarry, Machynlleth, Powys, Wales SY20 9AZ. (Demonstrates many practical applications of 'green' living.)

English Nature, Northminster House, Peterborough PE1 1UA. (Government body promoting nature conservation in England.)

WATCH, The Green, Witham Park, Lincoln LN5 7JR. (National environmental club for children and young people.)

The following three organizations are working to protect the environment. Each one campaigns on a wide range of important issues:
Friends of the Earth, 26-28 Underwood Street, London N1 7JQ, or Bonnington Mill, 70-72 Newhaven Road, Edinburgh EH6 5QG.

Greenpeace, 30-31 Islington Green, London N1 8XE.

World Wide Fund for Nature UK, Panda House, Weyside Park, Godalming, Surrey GU7 1XR.

BOOKS TO READ

Atlas of the Environment (Wayland, 1991)
Being Green Begins at Home Birkin, Gell & Beeby (Greenprint, 1990)
The *Conserving Our World* series (Wayland, 1989/90)
The *Green Detective* series (Wayland, 1991/2)
How to be a Friend of the Earth (Friends of the Earth, 1992)
How to be Green J Button (Century Hutchinson, 1989)
Lucy's World S. Weatherill (Two-Can, 1991)
The Young Green Consumer Guide J Elkington and J Hailes (Gollancz, 1990)
Where Does Rubbish Go? S Tahta (Usborne, 1991)
The Young Person's Guide to Saving the Planet D Silver and B Vallely (Virago, 1989)

INDEX

acid rain 8, 22, 24, 33, 46
action, local 5, 7, 9, 15, 20, 25, 27, 33, 44
aerosols 10
air pollution 6, 7, 22-9, 37
Amazon 9
Antarctic 26

baths 10, 11
batteries, rechargeable 33
beaches 26, 30, 33
buses 24
buying 'green' 6, 19, 21, 25, 44

campaigning 7, 44-5
cans 14, 21
carbon dioxide 37, 38, 46
carbon monoxide 24, 46
cars
  pollution 6, 7, 24, 32, 39
catalytic convertor 25, 46
CFCs 26, 27, 46
  recycling 15, 27, 28
Children's Crusade 4
Clean Air Act 23
compost 10, 21, 42
cycling 7, 22, 24

deforestation 4, 40-1
doorstep collections 18

energy
  efficiency 10, 38
  renewable 25, 46
  saving 6, 10, 11, 14, 25, 34, 35, 37
  use of 10, 11, 14, 34

fire extinguishers 27
flooding 37, 39
fossil fuels 23, 24, 29, 46
'Four Rs' of recycling 20
Friends of the Earth 41, 45
fundraising 9, 45
furniture 6, 15

gardens 21, 32, 42

glass
  reuse & recycling 17
global warming 7, 13, 37, 39, 46
government action 28
government targets 15
greenhouse effect 37, 46

habitats
  threatened 7, 8, 13, 14, 40-1
halons 26, 27, 46
hardwoods 10, 41
HCFCs 26
health risks 13, 22, 24, 25, 26, 29, 30, 31
home
  design of 34, 35
  use of energy 10
hydrocarbons 22, 32

insulation 10, 35, 36, 38

kitchen waste 17

landfill sites 12-13, 14
leachate 13
light bulbs 10
local action 5, 7, 9, 15, 20, 25, 27, 33, 44
local councils 15

metals 17
methane 13, 42

natural resources 14
newspapers
  recycling 14
nitrogen oxide 22, 24, 32, 46

ozone 22, 26, 46
ozone layer
  depletion of 26, 27, 28

packaging 10, 14, 20, 21
paper 13, 14, 17, 19
particulates
  test for 29
peatbogs 8, 9, 42

phosphates 30
plastics 17
pollution 32, 46
  air 6, 7, 22-9, 37
  reducing 6, 7, 14, 24, 25
  rivers and seas 13, 30, 32, 33
  water 8, 9, 13
ponds 44, 45
power stations 7
  pollution 7, 24, 25, 32
public transport 24, 28
pump-action sprays 10

rainforests 9, 40-1
recycled products
  toilet paper 10, 14, 19
  cost of 19
recycling 10, 21, 46
  at school 20
  cans 14, 21
  energy used 14
  facilities 15, 18
  paper 9, 13, 14, 19
renewable energy 25, 46
repair 16, 20, 21
reuse 14, 15, 16, 17, 20, 21, 46
rubbish 13
  around the world 16
  type of 17

sewage 30, 32, 46
showers 10, 11, 16
smogs 22, 23, 32, 46
sulphur dioxide 24, 32, 46

toilet paper 10, 14, 19
toxic waste 7
traffic jams 7
traffic pollution 10, 14, 24
tree of life 5
trees 22, 44

waste 14, 17
wildlife garden 42-3
wildlife under threat 8, 14, 40-1
wind power 25